DINKING
ALL DAY

DINKING
ALL
DAY

A PICKLEBALL
HANDBOOK *for the*
TRULY OBSESSED

Jamie Miller

CASTLE POINT BOOKS
NEW YORK

DINKING ALL DAY.
Copyright © 2024 by St. Martin's Press. All rights reserved.
Printed in China. For information, address St. Martin's Publishing Group,
120 Broadway, New York, NY 10271.

www.castlepointbooks.com

The Castle Point Books trademark is owned by Castle Point Publishing, LLC.
Castle Point books are published and distributed by St. Martin's Publishing Group.

ISBN 978-1-250-34709-1 (paper over board)
ISBN 978-1-250-34710-7 (ebook)

Editorial by Jen Calvert
Design by Melissa Gerber

Images used under license by Shutterstock.com.

Our books may be purchased in bulk for promotional, educational,
or business use. Please contact your local bookseller or the Macmillan
Corporate and Premium Sales Department at 1-800-221-7945, extension 5442,
or by email at MacmillanSpecialMarkets@macmillan.com.

First Edition: 2024

10 9 8 7 6 5 4 3 2 1

CONTENTS

introduction

Serving Smiles

Ask any pickler how they fell in love with the
game, and somewhere in their hour-long tale,
they'll tell you they weren't a fan at first. But
it's never long before the sport gets under your
skin. If that sounds familiar, you may be a Smash
Addict—or even a Drop-Shot Warrior—by now.
Dinking All Day raises a glass and a customized
paddle to your journey with all things pickleball:
helpful tips and trivia, hilarious quips, and,
of course, courtside cocktail recipes. (You've
found your people, and they are thirsty.)

phase 1

Sideline Skeptic

Does it sound like a game that first graders invented on the playground? Yes. Is it as fun as a game that first graders invented on the playground? Also yes. So how many self-respecting adults would play it? Oh, wait—36 million of them. And counting. But it's probably just a passing trend that will go the way of Jazzercise and the Thigh Master. Who needs exercise anyway? It's not like it's that good for you.

Crawl.
Walk.
Pickleball.

A PICKLEBALL CRASH COURSE

THE BALL HAS TO BOUNCE ONCE BEFORE YOU HIT IT.

GIVE YOUR PADDLE A HANDSHAKE, NOT A DEATH GRIP.

NO OVERHEAD WHACKING NEAR THE NET (THE NON-VOLLEY ZONE).

THE DINK (A SOFT, CONTROLLED SHOT DROPPED AT YOUR OPPONENT'S FEET) IS YOUR SECRET WEAPON.

NO SORE LOSERS ALLOWED.

THINK VOLLEYBALL, NOT TENNIS. UNDERHAND SERVES ONLY.

The couple that plays pickleball together . . . is probably going to need therapy.

TENNIS-OBSESSED TIM

WEARS A BLINDFOLD TO PLAY SO HE CAN SHOW OFF HIS ATHLETIC SUPERIORITY

FAVORITE PHRASE IS "DO YOU KNOW WHO I AM?"

REMINDS YOU PERIODICALLY THAT HE'S ONLY PLAYING PICKLEBALL IRONICALLY

HEMS ALL HIS SHORTS TO A 6-INCH INSEAM AND BLINDS PEOPLE WITH HIS PALE UPPER THIGHS

USES HOME ALONE-STYLE TRAPS TO CATCH PICKLEBALLERS THAT TRESPASS ON HIS COURTS

13

THE SPORTING GOODS STORE *is* HAVING *a* SALE *on* PICKLEBALL GEAR. BUT IT'S FIRST COME, FIRST SERVED.

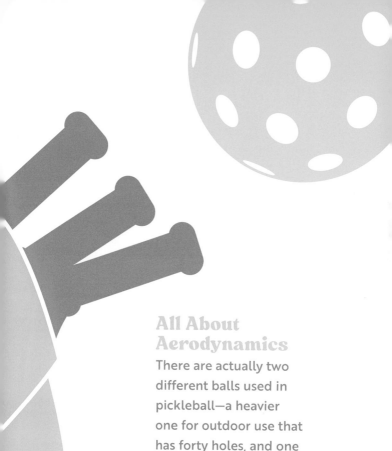

All About Aerodynamics

There are actually two different balls used in pickleball—a heavier one for outdoor use that has forty holes, and one for indoor use that has twenty-six wider holes.

Life is good. Pickleball makes it better.

THE BASELINE

· Serves 1 ·

A smashing blend of sporting spirit and classic cocktail flair, this elderflower-infused cocktail is the essence of pickleball. Sip it slowly and let it open your mind to the beauty of the game.

2–3 cucumber slices

3–4 fresh basil leaves

2 ounces gin

½ ounce elderflower liqueur

½ ounce fresh lemon juice

½ ounce simple syrup

Cucumber slice and basil sprig, for garnish

1. In a cocktail shaker, muddle the cucumber slices and basil leaves.

2. Add ice, followed by the gin, elderflower liqueur, fresh lemon juice, and simple syrup.

3. Shake and strain the mixture into a chilled martini glass.

4. Top it off with a splash of soda water and garnish with cucumber and basil.

"Despite its silly terms and funny name, pickleball is actually quite a sophisticated game."

—BILL GATES, SOPHISTICATED CREATOR OF MICROSOFT

SAY IT TO THEIR FACES

Think you're too cool for pickleball? Tell that to Lebron James, Jamie Foxx, George and Amal Clooney, Selena Gomez, Drew Brees, Serena Williams, and Billie Eilish. They all love the game.

BEDAZZLED PADDLES

It may seem like overkill to those who haven't yet accepted pickleball into their hearts, but there's a reason for customizing your stuff: namely, avoiding mix-ups. It gets a lot harder for someone to mistakenly grab your gear if it's covered in pictures of your face.

Top 5 Most Played Songs in Phase 1

"Wicked Game" *by* Chris Isaak

"Under Pressure" *by* Queen and David Bowie

"Never Surrender" *by* Corey Hart

"You Can't Hurry Love" *by* The Supremes

"Torn" *by* Natalie Imbruglia

My neighbor
told me his dog
found a pickleball
two miles away
from the nearest
courts. Sounds
far-fetched.

THE ORIGIN STORY

Congressman Joel Pritchard and his neighbor Bob S. O'Brian created pickleball out of boredom one sunny summer day in 1965 on Bainbridge Island, Washington. They used what they had on hand—a badminton court, Ping-Pong paddles, and a Wiffle ball—to create a family-friendly game. After cluing in fellow friend Barney McCallum, they made the game official with actual rules. And things snowballed very, very slowly from there!

THE HUMBLE
PICKLEBALL PADDLE:
TOOL, ACCESSORY,
SHIELD, AND
OCCASIONAL
FRISBEE, WHEN
MATCHES GET HEATED.

SPECTATOR SAM

DREAMS OF A DAY WHEN SOMEONE INVITES HER TO PLAY

LIVES IN THE SHADOWS, LIKE BATMAN, BUT YEARNS FOR HER TIME TO SHINE

ALWAYS GOT PICKED LAST IN GYM CLASS

WALKS HER DOG SLOWLY PAST EVERY PICKLEBALL COURT IN TOWN

READS PICKLEBALL CHAT BOARDS LIKE THEY'RE *PEOPLE* MAGAZINE

25

You're in the smash zone.

KISS THE BALL

Newbies tend to go hard, but experienced picklers know it's all about control. Keeping your serves simple and practiced ensures that the ball drops where you want it to. Focus on getting your forehand, backhand, and dink just right before trying any fancy new moves.

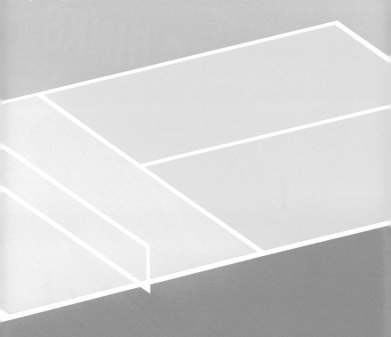

Now

SERVING

ICE-COLD DINKS.

THE PINK DINK

· Serves 2 ·

This refreshing beverage is both energizing and alcohol-free, allowing you to keep your head in the game. But if you're looking for a post-game pick-me-up, a little peach schnapps in place of the peach juice will do the trick.

2½ ounces peach juice

2½ ounces strawberry lemonade

1 tablespoon grenadine syrup

2½ ounces soda water

Peach slices and strawberries, for garnish

1. In a cocktail shaker filled with ice, combine the peach juice, strawberry lemonade, and grenadine.

2. Pour the mixture into two tall glasses. Top with more ice and add the soda water.

3. Garnish with the peaches and strawberries.

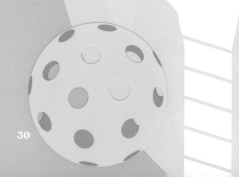

"I never thought I'd say this: as long as I can walk, I'm playing pickleball. I can't wait to get back on the court."

—ANDRE AGASSI, PRO TENNIS PLAYER

SOMETHING TO THIS

Pickleball is the fastest growing sport in America. And why wouldn't it be? This Frankenstein's monster created from tennis, Ping-Pong, badminton, and Wiffle ball is easy to pick up, fun to play, and challenging enough to make you want to score a win.

A Pickleball Limerick

There once was a pickler named Strunk,
Who thought he could win the game drunk;
He swung at the ball,
But instead took a fall,
And proved that his moves were all junk.

Playing Pickleball Improves Memory

WHAT'S THE SCORE?

WHO JUST SERVED?

WERE YOU 1 OR 2?

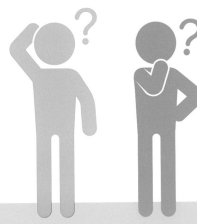

Pickleball is the avocado toast of sports—fun, healthy, and makes you say, "Where has this been all my life?"

GREAT MINDS DINK ALIKE

One of the best ways to not only learn pickleball but learn to love it is to recruit your friends. Nothing will get you into the spirit of this game like the pickleball community. After all, pickleball was invented to bring families together.

Kitchen's Closed.

SPIN AND TONIC

· Serves 1 ·

You know what goes great with an outdoor game played in beautiful, sunny weather? Delicious tropical fruit filled with antioxidants. And gin.

2 ounces gin

1 ounce pink guava puree

1 ounce lychee puree

¾ ounce lemon juice

Soda water

Lemon slice, for garnish

1. In a cocktail shaker filled with ice, combine the gin, guava puree, lychee puree, and lemon juice.

2. Shake and strain into a highball glass filled with ice.

3. Top with soda water and garnish with lemon.

phase 2

Pickleball Curious

Pickleball courts are popping up like coffee shops, you have to work around friends' matches to make plans, and brightly colored gear is taking over your social feeds. Maybe there's more to this pickleball thing than you thought. But you're not sold just yet. You need to get your hands on a paddle and see what all the fuss is about. Luckily, your neighbor Barb is more than happy to school you on the court. "Just give it time," she says. Just give it time.

PICKLEBALL: CHEAPER THAN THERAPY

AND WAY MORE FUN.

HISTORY of PICKLEBALL TIMELINE

1965: Creation of Pickleball

1967: First Pickleball Court

1972: Pickleball Corporation

1976: First Pickleball Tournament

1984: First Composite Pickleball Paddle

1984: United States Amateur Pickleball Association

1990: Pickleball Hits All 50 States

2022: Pickleball Goes Viral

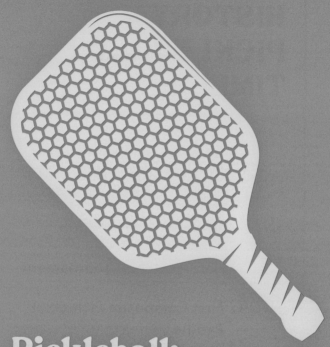

Pickleball:
the perfect blend of skill and absurdity.

PICKLED BLOODY MARY

• Serves 4 •

Whip up a pitcher of these beauties for after those early morning games and you'll be hailed as a hero.

Juice of 1 (14-ounce) jar cornichons (gherkins)

2 cups tomato juice

8 ounces vodka

2 tablespoons Worcestershire sauce

1 tablespoon horseradish

2 teaspoons hot sauce

Juice of ½ a large lemon, plus lemon wedge for rim

Freshly ground black pepper

3 tablespoons kosher salt

1 tablespoon chili powder

Cornichons, celery stalks, fresh dill, and lemon wedges, for garnish

1. Fill an ice tray with pickle juice and freeze.

2. In a large pitcher, combine the tomato juice, vodka, Worcestershire, horseradish, hot sauce, lemon juice, and pepper.

3. Combine the salt and chili powder on a small plate. Run a lemon wedge around the rim of four highball glasses and dip them in the salt mixture.

4. Add the pickle-juice ice cubes and Bloody Mary mixture to the glasses and garnish.

What do you call a dinosaur with a Wiffle ball?

A dinkosaurus.

PUT YOUR SHOULDER INTO IT

Dinking gets a lot of hate as a newbie move, but these soft shots that stay close to the net can be the key to winning. The trick is forcing your opponent out of position by making them reach for the ball, and that means keeping your wrist and elbow straight while lifting your shoulder to control your swing.

"For me, joy + play = pickleball. I'm obsessed and try to play four to five times a week. The court might be the only place in the world where I'm fully in the now."

—BRENÉ BROWN, AUTHOR AND OWNER OF ATX PICKLEBALLERS MAJOR LEAGUE PICKLEBALL TEAM

Top 5 Most Played Songs in Phase 2

"Give Me a Reason" *by* Pink

"Light My Fire" *by* The Doors

"Wouldn't It Be Nice" *by* The Beach Boys

"Could It Be I'm Falling in Love"
   by The Spinners

"Maybe I'm Amazed" *by* Paul McCartney

PICKLEBALL PLAYER: *(n.)*

Similar to a tennis player, but cooler. (See also *awesome*)

THE
Unwritten
RULES

As with any sport, there's an understood code of conduct in pickleball.

1. Pickleballs are wiley. Always alert others to wayward Wiffles by yelling, "Ball on the court!"

2. If you've got next, place your paddle in the provided holders.

3. Never leave a player hanging when they go for the congratulatory paddle tap.

Got it!
Oops. Yours.

BEER 🤝 PICKLEBALL

Anheuser-Busch (brewers of beer, owners of Clydesdales) purchased a Major League Pickleball team for seven figures in 2022. They're the first Fortune 500 company to get in on the game officially.

My job drives me to dink.

THE EASY BRUISER

YELPS IN FEAR IF YOU SWING A PADDLE NEAR HIM

WENT FOR A DARING ERNE SHOT AND WAS NEVER THE SAME

BUYS ATHLETIC TAPE IN BULK

HAS SEEN THE MOVIE *UNBREAKABLE* SEVENTEEN TIMES

INSTALLED A COLD PLUNGE TUB IN HIS BACK YARD, THEN PULLED A MUSCLE GETTING IN

53

A Pickleball Haiku

I love to slam hard—
But sometimes I miss the ball,
And fall on my face.

PICKLED SHANDY

· Serves 10 ·

There's no crying in pickleball. But if you do feel the need to cry into your beer over a shutout game, this is the one. And because sharing is caring, this recipe makes enough grapefruit-ginger juice for ten drinks.

4 cups fresh grapefruit juice, chilled
¼ cup finely chopped pickled ginger
¼ cup pickled ginger juice
Pinch kosher salt
¼–½ teaspoon freshly ground black pepper
Light lager

1. In a large cocktail shaker, combine the grapefruit juice, pickled ginger, pickled ginger juice, salt, and pepper.

2. Strain the grapefruit-ginger juice evenly between tulip or pint glasses with ice. Hold the glasses at a slight angle to control the foam and top each off with an ice-cold lager.

Top 5 Reasons You Start Playing Pickleball

1. It looked easy
2. Your wife/friend/boss made you
3. It looked like fun
4. You suffer from FOMO
5. Your competitive streak knows no bounds

WHAT'S IN A NAME?

Contrary to popular belief (spurred on by Joel Pritchard himself), pickleball was not named after the family dog. Instead, Pritchard's wife, Joan, came up with the name after comparing the newly created hodgepodge of a sport to the "pickle boat" in crew—a team of leftover non-starters. The dog came along later, and they named him Pickles after the family game.

A PICKLEBALL SITS DOWN AT THE BAR.

THE BARTENDER ASKS, "HAVE YOU BEEN SERVED?"

FEET FIRST

Beginning picklers and pros alike can get so engrossed in the game that they forget this all-important mantra: feet first. Moving your feet mid-swing can cost you the shot, so make sure you watch the ball, get your feet into position, and then swing.

I'd
hit
that.

PICKLEBALL is HIGH-TECH

The first official pickleball paddles designed for the sport were created by Boeing Industrial Engineer Arlen Paranto, who made his from fiberglass and honeycomb Nomex panels that are also used in the flooring and structural systems of commercial airplanes.

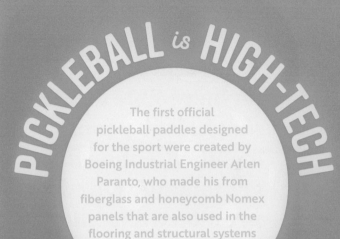

> **"We see pickleball as an incredible medium that brings people together, connects communities, and promotes a healthy and active lifestyle."**
>
> —DREW BREES, NFL QUARTERBACK

ONE, TWO, THREE, SMASH

Since the first two shots have to bounce, good strategy is all about that third shot. You can dink or drive, but the goal is the same: get to the kitchen (the non-volley zone by the net). That's where games are won or lost. Which you choose depends on which you do better, but if you go with a drive, make sure you only give it about 80 percent of your power to avoid hitting it out of bounds.

It's a good day to play pickleball!

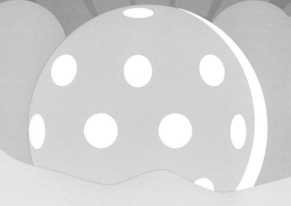

SMACK-TALKING TREVOR

AFTER TROUNCING HIS GRANDMA IN A MATCH, TOLD HER SHE "SHOULD HAVE COME TO PLAY"

WILL DO A DRAMATIC DIVING ROLL FOR A DEAD BALL

KEEPS HIS JUNIOR TENNIS LEAGUE PARTICIPATION TROPHY IN A LIGHTED CASE

DRINKS FITNESS SHAKES MADE FROM THE BLOOD, SWEAT, AND TEARS OF HIS RIVALS

INVENTED A VIRAL TIKTOK DANCE CALLED "THE THIRD SHOT DROP"

DINK RESPONSIBLY. DON'T GET SMASHED.

CAN'T FEEL MY (PADDLE) FACE

• Serves 2 •

Ready to take things up a notch? Ginger liqueur and jalapeño add a kick to this refreshing cucumber-based cocktail. But as in pickleball, you can always pull back if you can't take the heat.

3 ounces tequila

1½ ounces fresh lime juice

½ ounce agave nectar

½ ounce ginger liqueur

½ cup pineapple juice

¼ cup cucumber juice

Splash sparkling white wine

Fresh cucumber and jalapeño slices, for garnish

1. In a cocktail shaker filled with ice, combine tequila, lime juice, agave nectar, ginger liqueur, pineapple juice, and cucumber juice.

2. Shake and distribute the mixture into two pint glasses filled with ice.

3. Top each glass with sparkling wine and garnish with cucumber and jalapeño slices.

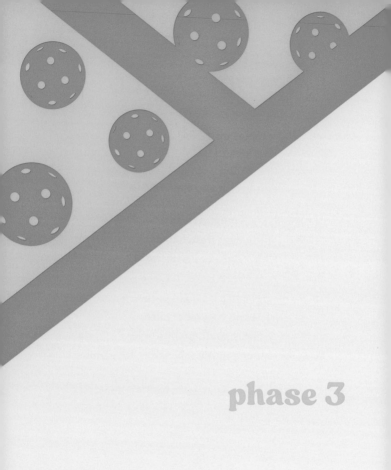

phase 3

Dink Devotee

One game in, you're in love. Suddenly, you're buying custom gear and forsaking your other hobbies. Have you binged the latest episodes of that soothing baking show? Of course not. You've been busy winning your own trophies—or at least, bragging rights at the bar after the game. The sky is bluer, the courts are greener, the air is sweeter, and you're ready to take on the world. . . until you have to leave for work. But you'll be back, champ.

IN MY
PICKLEBALL ERA.

GOING PRO
HAS ITS PERKS

The best picklers in the major leagues can make up to $250,000 a year with sponsorship deals.

I'll dink to that!

MAKE IT A DOUBLE

· Serves 2 ·

Stiff muscles require stiffer drinks. Reward yourself
and your better half for going all in with this extra-
strong old fashioned, après pickleball match.

8 ounces bourbon whiskey
8 dashes orange bitters
2 ounces simple syrup
2 large ice cubes
Maraschino cherries and orange peels, for garnish

1. Divide the whiskey between two double old
   fashioned glasses. Add 4 ounces of orange bitters
   and 1 ounce of simple syrup to each glass and stir
   using a bar spoon.

2. Add an ice cube, a cherry, and a piece of orange peel
   to each glass, and serve.

"She kills me—
if we play six
games, I'll win
maybe two."

—GEORGE CLOONEY,
PICKLEBALL AFFICIONADO,
ON HIS WIFE, AMAL

DIVORCE ALLEY: (n.)

The no-man's land between two players on the same team that can lead to arguments when both go for the ball.

Dinking of you.

X ♥ X ♥

Top 5 Most Played Songs in Phase 3

"Sweet Surrender" *by* Sarah McLachlan

"Heaven Is a Place on Earth" *by* Belinda Carlisle

"About Damn Time" *by* Lizzo

"Baby One More Time" *by* Britney Spears

"Look What You Made Me Do" *by* Taylor Swift

Sorry tennis, I'm with pickleball now.

PRACTICE MAKES PICKLERS

Drills are the key to leveling up your game. The more you practice, the more you'll learn to control your swing and predict where the ball will land.

I would,
but I have
pickleball.

THE DAIRY QUEEN

PLAYS A PLAIN VANILLA GAME, BUT WITH A DANGEROUS TWIST

RETURNS THE BALL SO FAST YOU GET A CRIPPLING HEADACHE

DELIVERS A SOFT SERVE THAT GIVES HER OPPONENT CHILLS

WILL ONLY HAND THINGS TO PEOPLE ON THE DIAGONAL

SPENDS ALL WEEK CHASING THE HIGH OF AN AROUND-THE-POST SHOT

NEVER UNDERESTIMATE
an OLD MAN *with a*
PICKLEBALL PADDLE.

A LITTLE COMPETITION

The largest pickleball tournament in the world—called the Minto U.S. Open Pickleball Championships—draws thousands of people and is appropriately held in the retirement capital of the United States: Naples, Florida.

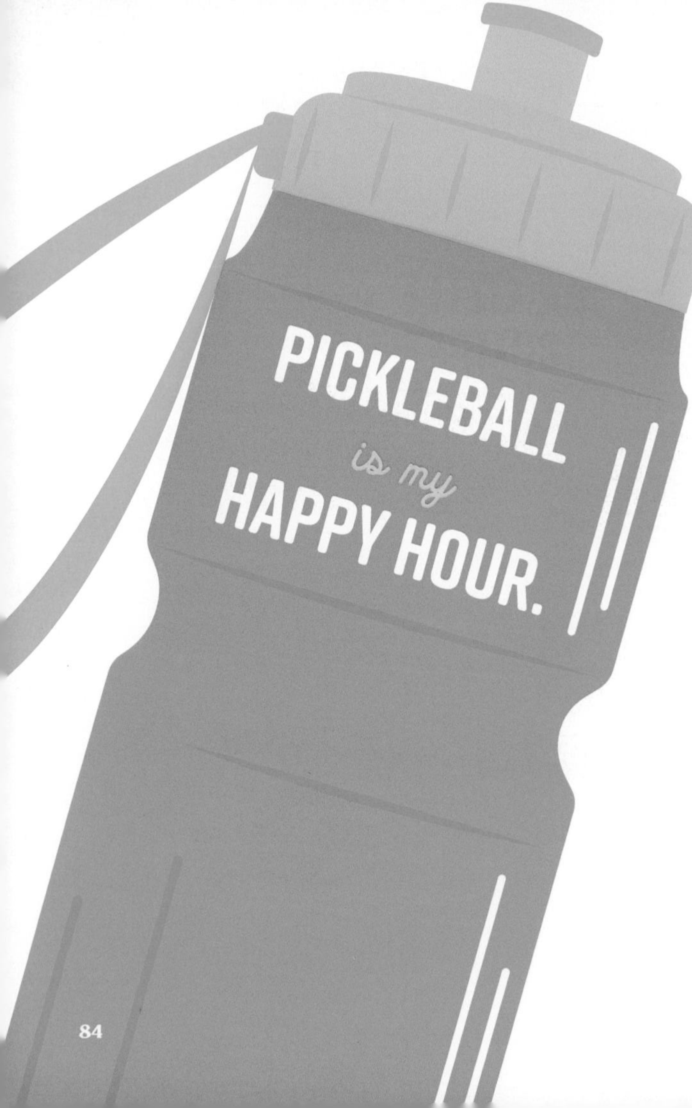
PICKLEBALL
is my
HAPPY HOUR.

THE BAINBRIDGE ISLAND ZINGER

· Serves 4 ·

This tasty ode to the birthplace of pickleball is everything its inventors intended the sport to be—bright, energizing, and intoxicating if enjoyed in excess. (But you can skip the bourbon and it'll be just as delightful.)

½ cup sugar

1¼ cups cold water, divided

Juice and zest of 1 lemon

4 cups berry zinger tea brewed with 2 teabags, cooled

4 ounces bourbon

Crushed ice

1. To make the lemon simple syrup: In a small saucepan over medium heat, stir together the sugar, ¼ cup of the water, lemon juice, and zest. Bring the mixture to a simmer and stir until the sugar has dissolved completely. Remove the pan from the heat and let the mixture cool.

2. In a large pitcher, stir together the brewed tea with the lemon simple syrup and remaining water. Stir in the bourbon, if desired, and divide the mixture between four glasses filled with crushed ice.

Life Is Full of Choices

Work
Pickleball

Pickleball

Pickleball

Pickleball

Family Reunion

Family Reunion

Pickleball at the Family Reunion

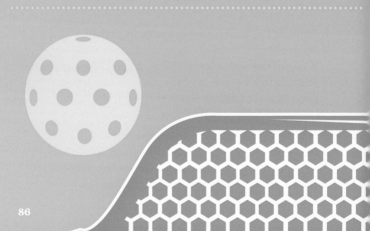

JUST DINK IT

Don't overthink your shots. In pickleball, hesitation can cost you. So practice, practice, practice, but then trust your skills.

RETIRED: *(adj.)*
The ability to play
pickleball whenever
and wherever I want.
(See also *fanatic*)

CHANGING THE GAME

Although pickleball used to be a retiree's game, its demographics have changed. There are as many players over the age of sixty-five as there are under the age of thirty-four, but most picklers fall somewhere in between the two.

A Pickleball Couplet

In pickleball's embrace,
we reach for the win,

With our every move,
we make heads and balls spin.

RULE-OBSESSED RORY

GOT HIS NEPHEW BANNED FROM THE LEAGUE FOR SERVING OVERHAND

CHECKS HIS DRONE FOOTAGE WHEN SOMEONE STEPS NEAR THE LINE

MAKES HIS DOG OBSERVE THE DOUBLE-BOUNCE RULE WHEN PLAYING FETCH

SIGNALS BEFORE TURNING INTO HIS OWN DRIVEWAY

HAS HIS WHITE-NOISE APP SET TO DINKING

"On the same court, you can have a millionaire with someone living paycheck to paycheck. No one's interested in what you do for a living, only in how long you've been playing."

—SIMONE JARDIM,
   PRO PICKLEBALL PLAYER

PICKLEBALL EMERGENCY KIT

BANDAGES

VODKA

DEODORANT

HAIR TIE

IBUPROFEN

SUNSCREEN

I'M OK WITH MY PICKLEBALL
DOUBLES PARTNER
POACHING MY SHOTS,
BUT WE WERE IN A BAR.

YOURS, MINE, AND OURS

In pickleball doubles as in all relationships, communication is key. Deciding ahead of time who will go for the balls that come down the middle (and what constitutes the "middle") can save you from missed balls and arguments. And let the faster partner take the lobs.

DESIGNATED DINKER

THE VOLLEY LLAMA

• Serves 1 •

This refreshing blend of tequila, agave, and lime is perfect
for cooling down after a spirited (read: exhausting)
match. A water chaser couldn't hurt, though.

2 ounces tequila blanco
1 ounce fresh lime juice
½ ounce agave syrup
3 ounces soda water
Pinch salt
Lime wheel, for garnish

1. In a cocktail shaker filled with ice, combine the
   tequila, lime juice, agave syrup, and salt.
2. Shake and strain the mixture into a highball glass
   filled with ice.
3. Top it up with club soda and garnish with the lime.

phase 4

Smash Addict

Pickleball is more than just a game to you. Pickleball is life. From your monogrammed pickleball bag and protein-packed charcuterie platter to your rigorous practice schedule, you take the sport seriously. As far as you're concerned, it's always a good day for a match. You'll go to your nephew's birthday party next year. Or better yet, you'll teach him how to play. Is there a better present than pickleball? Rhetorical question.

Eat.
Sleep.
Pickleball.
Repeat.

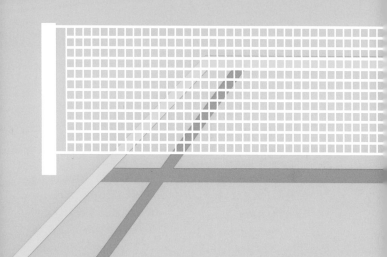

A NATURAL HIGH

You're not crazy (probably)—pickleball really
is addictive. Its low entry point, scalability, and
high reward are designed to make you want
more. Plus, being active in nature with others
gives you a nice little dink shot of dopamine.

SET GOALS

There's always room for improvement, so keep doing drills and practicing your shots. But remember, this is supposed to be fun! Unless you're going pro (and not just fantasizing about it), don't put too much pressure on yourself.

Why I Lose at Pickleball

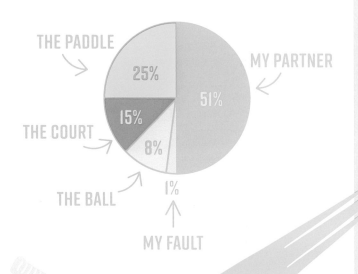

THE PADDLE
25%

MY PARTNER
51%

THE COURT
15%

THE BALL
8%

MY FAULT
1%

EVERYTHING *in* MODERATION

EXCEPT PICKLEBALL AND WINE.

PICKLEBALL SPRITZ

· **Serves 1** ·

The perfect way to quench your thirst after—or during—a marathon of matches, this spritz is best when made with a fruity table wine. Bring your cocktails courtside by adding all of the ingredients to a large portable pitcher.

4 ounces red wine

4 ounces sparkling lemonade

Lemon and orange wheels

Mint, for garnish (optional)

1. In a large glass filled with ice, combine the red wine and sparkling lemonade.

2. Give the lemon and orange wheels a twist before stirring into the glass.

3. Garnish with mint, if desired, before serving.

Why did the pickleball player have to break up with his tennis-playing girlfriend? Love meant nothing to him.

Top 5 Most Played Songs in Phase 4

"Hard to Explain" by The Strokes

"Never Gonna Give You Up" by Rick Astley

"Love Is a Battlefield" by Pat Benatar

"Don't Stop 'Til You Get Enough"
by Michael Jackson

"The Edge of Glory" by Lady Gaga

TEARS *of my* PICKLEBALL OPPONENTS.

SCORE-KEEPING SUSAN

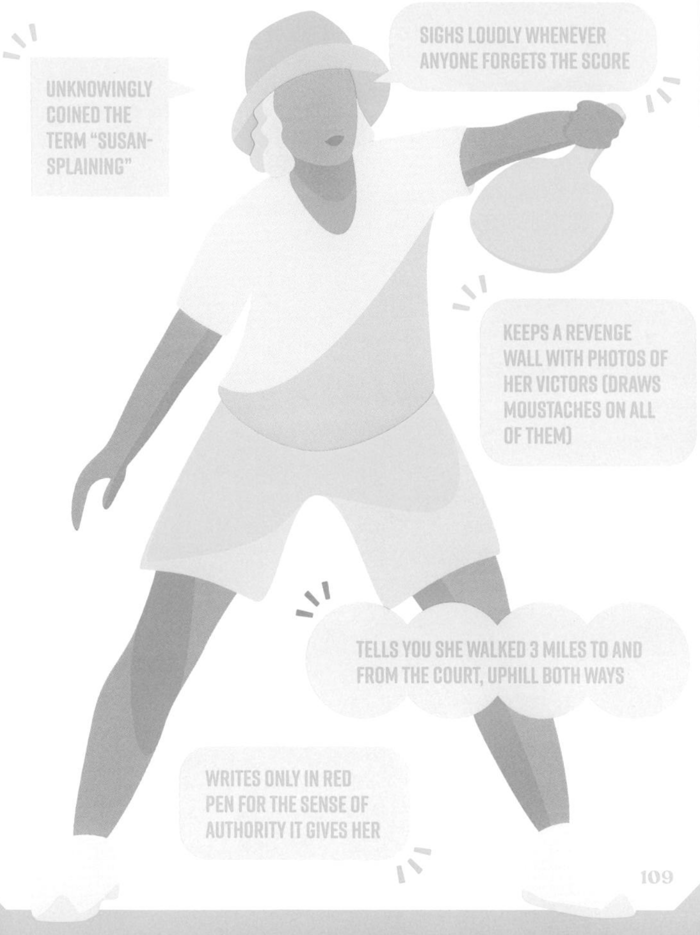

It's *always* pickleball season.

SWITCHING TEAMS

Retired football quarterback Tom Brady is now part-owner of a Major League Pickleball team. And he's not the only one. Drew Brees, Patrick Mahomes, LeBron James, Kevin Durant, Draymond Green, Kevin Love, Naomi Osaka, and James Blake have all invested in the sport.

"You've got to be able to hit the ball hard. Nobody plays golf to putt."

—JOEL PRITCHARD, CO-CREATOR OF PICKLEBALL

THINGS I DO IN MY SPARE TIME

Play Pickleball!

Watch Others Play Pickleball

Research Pickleball

Talk about Pickleball

Dream about Pickleball

I LOVE PICKLEBALL!

PUNCH VOLLEY PUNCH

· Serves 2 ·

Just like the punch shot, this winning drink is deceptively powerful despite being compact. If spiced rum is a little too much power for you, swap in clear light rum for a softer version of the cocktail.

2 ounces dark pineapple rum

1 ounce spiced rum

1 ounce Falernum liqueur

1 ounce peach liqueur

½ ounce lime juice

½ ounce lemon juice

2 dashes Peychaud's bitters

1 dash aromatic bitters

Crushed ice

1 pineapple wedge, for garnish

1. In a cocktail shaker filled with crushed ice, combine the liquid ingredients.

2. Shake and strain the mixture into two rocks glasses filled with crushed ice, and garnish.

I don't always play pickleball.

...Oh, wait, yes I do.

TALK ABOUT ADDICTED

The longest official pickleball match on record lasted thirteen hours and fifteen minutes during the 2013 USAPA National Championships. But the Guinness World Record belongs to Matt Chambers and Alex Bean for a twenty-four-hour game in 2021.

"THE MAIN THING IN PICKLEBALL IS TO BE PATIENT. BE PATIENT WHILE BEING EXTREMELY AGGRESSIVE WITH YOUR LEGS. YOU NEED TO GET LOW AND BE ABLE TO DINK FOR HOURS TO WAIT FOR THE BALL THAT IS HIGH AND PUT IT AWAY."

—CATHERINE PARENTEAU, PRO PICKLEBALL PLAYER

LOBS ARE FOR WINNERS

Don't be afraid to use the lob shot when your opponents are at the net. Remember, lobbing is not a sign of weakness—it's a smart strategy to keep your opponents guessing. A well-placed lob can catch them off-guard and force them to scramble back to the baseline. Just be careful not to hit the lob too high or too short, or you might end up giving them an easy smash.

An Ode to Pickleball

Work piles high, profits are lost,

But on the pickleball court, I'm finally the boss.

Emails and tasks, they all lose their places,

'Cause who needs a job when you're serving up aces?

CHEATING CHAD

VENMOS HIS LEAGUE FEES MINUS THE AAA DISCOUNT HE OFFERS HIMSELF

SCREAMS OUT, "I WASN'T READY!" EVERY TIME SOMEONE SERVES

SELLS THE WATER BOTTLES AND SUNGLASSES PEOPLE LEAVE BEHIND ON EBAY

GREASES HIS PADDLE WITH COOKING OIL BEFORE EACH MATCH

WEARS 2-INCH LIFTS IN HIS COURT SHOES BUT WILL GO TO THE GRAVE DENYING IT

121

Q: Why did you charge the pickleball net?

A: Because I was out of cash.

NASTY NELSON: *(n.)*

A vicious serve that purposely hits the non-receiving person on the opposing team. It scores one for the serving team, but at the cost of your integrity.

You might be a pickleball addict
IF YOU OWN MORE PADDLES
THAN PAIRS OF CLEAN UNDERWEAR.

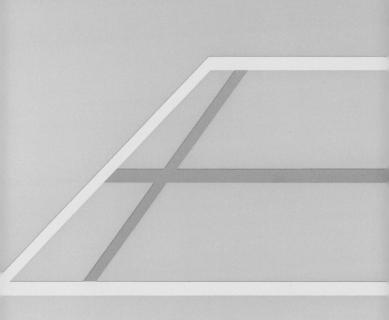

LEVEL UP YOUR GAME

They say you are the sum of the people you surround yourself with, and nowhere is that truer than in sports. Want to level up your pickleball game? Play picklers who are better than you are. It's really that simple. When you challenge yourself, you learn and grow. (You also lose a lot. But it's for a good cause!)

If you can't take the heat, stay out of the kitchen.

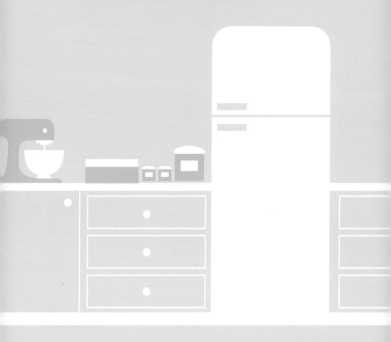

THE KITCHEN SINK

· Serves 4 ·

Leave the Long Island Iced Tea for the tennis players—this bright and invigorating twist on the classic is tailor-made for picklers. With mint, lime, and citrus, it's good to a fault.

4 sprigs fresh mint
2 ounces simple syrup
2 ounces gin
2 ounces vodka
2 ounces light rum
2 ounces triple sec
8 ounces lemon seltzer
4 lime wedges, for garnish

1. In a cocktail shaker, muddle the mint. Add ice and combine the simple syrup, gin, vodka, light rum, and triple sec.

2. Shake and strain the mixture into highball glasses filled with ice. Top each with the seltzer and garnish with a lime wedge.

phase 5

Drop-Shot Warrior

You've reached a Zen-like place in your game. When you're on the court, all the chatter fades away, you and your partner move as one, and your drop shots flow as easily as the sports drinks you pour over your own head in victory. You could go pro, but what's the point? You know you're the best. You don't need paparazzi getting in the way of your sacred game time. Ommm . . .

I dink, therefore I AM.

BIG DINK ENERGY

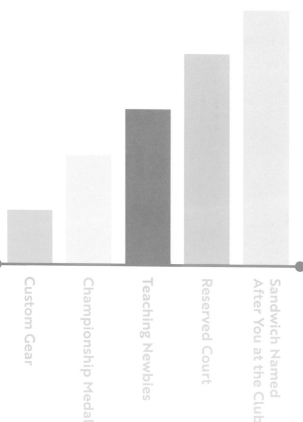

Custom Gear

Championship Medal

Teaching Newbies

Reserved Court

Sandwich Named After You at the Club

What's mine is yours—except middle balls on my forehand. Those are mine.

SHOWOFF SHAUNA

SHOUTS "GET OUT OF THE KITCHEN" TO ANYONE IN HER ACTUAL KITCHEN

FOUNDING MEMBER OF THE VOLLEY LLAMAS

TOSSES HER SWEATY TOWEL TO CONFUSED PASSERSBY, MISTAKING THEM FOR DIE-HARD FANS

PUTS A TOPSPIN ON THE REMOTE WHEN SHE PASSES IT TO HER HUSBAND

JINGLES ONTO THE COURT CARRYING EVERY ONE OF HER MEDALS IN HER GEAR BAG.

133

Peace, Love, and Pickleball

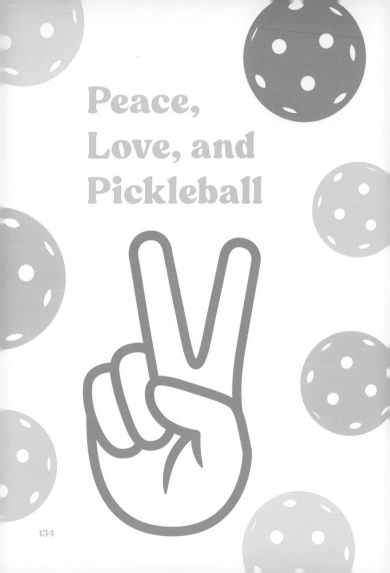

ERNE COLLINS

· Serves 1 ·

Just like an Erne (an advanced shot for which you jump the kitchen), this cocktail is tricky. It's not difficult, but it does change color thanks to the gin's butterfly pea flower. And both the shot and the cocktail are meant to be savored.

2 ounces Empress 1908 Indigo gin

½ ounce lavender simple syrup

Ice

1 ounce lemon juice

Splash soda water

Edible flowers, for garnish

1. Combine the gin and simple syrup in a carafe and pour the mixture into a Collins glass over ice.

2. Slowly pour in the lemon juice, and stir to combine.

3. Top the drink off with soda water and garnish it with edible flowers.

Probably *playing* pickleball.

A SPORT WITHOUT BORDERS

Pickleball isn't a strictly American sport. The International Pickleball Federation (IPF) was created in 2010 to regulate and promote the sport across the world and boasts seventy-six member countries.

A day without pickleball probably wouldn't kill me. But why risk it?

DIG DOWN DEEP

If you want to be a Drop Shot Warrior, you need to learn how to reset the ball during a fast rally so you can finish your opponent off with an unattackable ball. Get that low bounce with a dig, keeping your paddle low and your split stance wide.

I PLAY PICKLEBALL BECAUSE PUNCHING PEOPLE IS FROWNED UPON.

ALL-INCLUSIVE

At its heart, Pickleball is all about inclusivity. Not only does the sport span genders and generations, it's also accessible to players with disabilities.

"Turns out that bending your knees in pickleball is just straight magic."

—BEN JOHNS, PRO PICKLEBALL PLAYER

CHAMPION SHOT

· Serves 1 ·

If you're the kind of pickler to go for the champion shot (a double-bouncer in the NVZ), this drop shot is for you. The trick is to throw back the drink with the same fervor that you hit that ball.

¾ ounce raspberry liqueur

½ ounce vodka

4 ounces berry-flavored energy drink or hard cider

1. Combine the raspberry liqueur and vodka in a shot glass.

2. Pour the energy drink into a pint or rocks glass.

3. Drop the shot glass into the other glass and drink it quickly.

SMELLS LIKE SWEAT *and* VICTORY.

I'm the Legend.
It's Me.

On the pickleball court,
I stand,
a player in the moment,
a master of the game.
The soft dinks,
the thundering smashes,
the rhythm of strategy and finesse . . .
In the world of pickleball,
I am the G.O.A.T.

"**My pickleball motto, however, is** Rip, Bang, Win, Cake! **Rip the ball, bang the ball, win the match, and celebrate with cake!**"

—ANNALEIGH WATERS,
PRO PICKLEBALL PLAYER

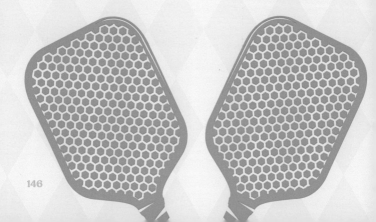

IT'S ALL IN THE WRIST

Expert-level flicking requires nimble wrists, which you can get by using hand grip–strengthening devices. Will you look silly answering "pickleball" to anyone who asks why you're training your grip? Yes. Will it be worth it when you flick your way to victory? Also yes.

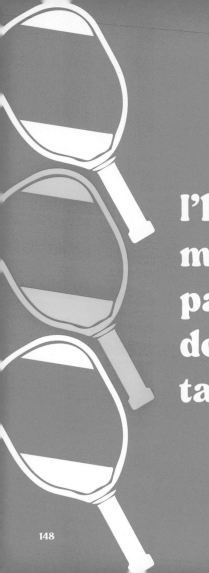

I'll let my paddle do the talking.

DO LESS

To reach that Zen place occupied by true drop-shot warriors, you need to remember that less is more. Take your time, think strategically, and move thoughtfully. A subtle flick of the wrist can be mightier than a full-throated smash.

Behind every man who misses a poach is his mixed partner glaring at him.

GEAR-OBSESSED GARY

HAS NAMES FOR ALL OF HIS CUSTOM PADDLES AND HAS HIS FAVORITE TATTOOED ON HIS SHIN

TROLLS INSTAGRAM POSTS TO TRASH-TALK PEOPLES' PICKLEBALL BAGS

ALTERED HIS WILL TO INCLUDE BEING BURIED IN HIS PICKLEBALL PERFORMANCE POLO

INSTALLED A GEAR RACK IN HIS WIFE'S OFFICE

OWNS OVERPRICED COURT SHOES SIGNED BY BEN JOHNS

THE GOLDEN PICKLE

The Golden Pickle is the ultimate achievement in pickleball: a perfect game. This happens when the first team to serve wins using that first serve and the opposing team never has a chance to serve.

Things to Do After Pickleball

- ✓ Stretch those hamstrings
- ✓ Hydrate (cocktails count)
- ✓ Review game tape
- ✓ Shop for new paddles
- ✓ Hit the message boards

PLAYING DRESS-UP

Although many sports, such as tennis, have an official dress code, Pickleball does not. Yet. So enjoy the freedom of athleisure while you can.

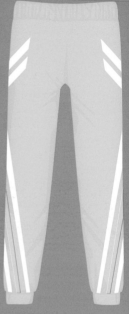

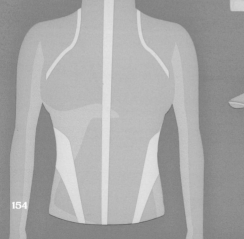

Top 5 Most Played Songs in Phase 5

"Levitating" *by* Dua Lipa

"We Are the Champions" *by* Queen

"Mama Said Knock You Out *by* LL Cool J

"Drop It Like It's Hot" *by* Snoop Dogg

"All I Do Is Win" *by* DJ Khaled

Keep calm *and* pickle on

THE BIG DILL

· Serves 2 ·

This cocktail takes everything that's great about a pickleback shot—namely whiskey (or bourbon) and pickle juice—and makes it worthy of a pickleball master. After all, you're a big dill.

4 ounces whiskey or bourbon

3 ounces pickle juice brine

1½ ounces fresh lime juice

1 ounce simple syrup

Dill pickle spear and fresh dill, for garnish

1. Stir together the whiskey, pickle juice, lime juice, and simple syrup.

2. Divide the mixture between two cocktail glasses filled with ice and garnish each with a pickle spear and fresh dill.

World's Greatest Pickleball Player

Glossary

ACE: A serve that the opponent cannot return.

APPROACH SHOT: A shot that you hit while moving toward the net.

BACKHAND: A shot that you hit on the opposite side of your dominant hand.

BASELINE: The line that marks the back end of the court.

CARRY: A shot that is not allowed, where the ball moves with your paddle rather than bouncing off it.

CENTERLINE: The line from the net to the baseline that divides the court into two equal halves.

CHOP: A shot that puts backspin on the ball, making it bounce low and slow. It's done by slicing the paddle from high to low.

CROSS-COURT: A shot that goes diagonally across the court.

DINK: A soft shot that barely goes over the net and lands in the non-volley zone.

DOUBLES: A game where four players play in two teams of two.

DOUBLE BOUNCE: A rule that applies to the first two shots of each rally and says each team must let the ball bounce once before hitting it.

DOUBLE HIT: A shot that is not allowed, where the ball hits your paddle twice or both you and your partner hit it.

DOWN THE LINE: A shot that goes straight along the sideline.

DRIVE: A hard and fast shot that goes deep into the opponent's court.

DROP SHOT: A soft shot that goes over the net and drops close to it.

FAULT: A mistake that ends the rally and gives the point to the other team.

FOREHAND: A shot that you hit on the same side of your dominant hand.

LOB: A high and deep shot that goes over your opponent's head.

NON-VOLLEY ZONE (AKA KITCHEN): The area near the net from which you cannot hit the ball without it bouncing first.

OVERHEAD SMASH: A powerful shot that you hit in the air above your head.

POACH: A move where you cross over to your partner's side and hit the ball:

RALLY: The exchange of shots between teams during a point. It starts with a serve and ends with a fault or a winner.

SERVE: The shot that starts each rally.

SIDELINE: The line that marks the side edge of the court.

SINGLES: A game where two players play against each other.

SLICE: A shot that puts spin on the ball, making it curve or bounce differently.

SWITCH: A move where you and your partner change sides during a rally.

THIRD SHOT DROP: A shot that you hit after the serve and the return, usually a drop shot that lands in the non-volley zone.

VOLLEY: A shot that you hit in the air before the ball bounces.